JUST BELOW THE SURFACE

*Poems Uncovering the Puzzles of Life
and Honoring the Joys of Family*

RICH WILBUR

DENVER, COLORADO

The tide recedes, but leaves behind
Bright seashells in the sand

The sun goes down, but gentle warmth
Still lingers on the land

The music stops, and yet
It echoes on in sweet refrains

For every joy that passes,
Something beautiful remains

Unknown author (found in R. Frost book)

To Edwin and Rosemary Wilbur whose steadfast love was the joy of their family of eight children

Contents

Introduction

A life in law makes one acutely aware of the beauty and utility of words. For most lawyers, words and books become central to our vocation and occasionally to our avocation – consider the explosion of legal novels authored by lawyers at the end of the last century, initiated by Scott Turow and moved forward by John Grisham. And some lawyers have been great writers – Lincoln for sure, but also jurists like Justices Holmes and Cardozo, and Judge Learned Hand. Holmes once advised that "a word is not a crystal, transparent and unchanged, but the skin of a living thought," wisdom enshrined in words more typical of poetry than law. While the immortals are few, many good lawyers write well and yet a life focused on verbal precision is an unlikely path to a passion for poetry. Mine arrived late in life.

Since prose is the basic medium of communication in law, politics, business, medicine, education, literature – indeed in life – one may ask why we need poetry. Poetry is unnecessary in a utilitarian sense, for directions to a hotel, to write a contract, draft a speech, or describe an event. In April 1865, an endless stream of words announced the assassination of our greatest President, Abraham Lincoln, to the grief-stricken nation. But Walt Whitman's poems "When Lilacs Last in the Dooryard Bloom'd" and "O Captain! My Captain!" told the story for eternity. We recently emerged from the bloodiest century in history, including WWI and WWII; men love history, especially the history of war, and many good accounts of those wars were best sellers, including Barbara Tuchman's *The Guns of August* and William Shirer's *The Rise and Fall of the Third Reich*. But has the sheer awfulness of war ever been captured as plainly and poignantly as in Wilfred Owen's great WWI poem *Dulce et Decorum Est*? We need poetry to account for the most intense human experiences: the bewildering, the devastating, and the simply beautiful. We need poetry for the human soul.

A poem is an existential response of the soul to the external world. "This is my letter to the World that never wrote to Me" begins a poem by perhaps America's greatest poet, Emily Dickinson. In telling a story, poetry speaks to the emotions, hints of music, uses cadence and rhythm, and tells the story with metaphors that sear and soar. Both music and metaphor are important in speaking to the soul – Robert Frost advised us to read poetry with our ears.

Emily Dickinson begins another poem with this line: "Hope is the thing with feathers that perches in the soul and sings the tune without the words and never stops at all." The very first word "Hope" tells us what the poem is about, and in the fourth word, hope is designated a "thing," enabling its full meaning to develop through a series of metaphors: the thing has "feathers" and it "perches" in the soul, telling us that from its home in the soul it can soar with the wind. Those two words strongly hint that hope is, in the ultimate metaphor, a bird. The word "bird" appears only once and once is enough for a genius. This bird can thrill as well as soar, for it "sings the tune without the words and never stops at all." There is a synergy when words are wedded to music, the senior partner in this combination. We sing an emotionally uplifting song in our morning shower and as the words slip from memory, we "sing the tune without the words." Hope continues to soar as we sing on. You could look for a century and not find a more powerful opening sentence to a poem – it takes several readings to sink in, to soar and thrill the soul. You learn more about a luscious piece of dark chocolate by letting it slowly dissolve in your mouth; poetry is best absorbed in a similar manner.

Poetry is incurably infected with the events of life. The poems that interest me the most – both those I write and those I read -- express philosophical concerns about the puzzles of life: the angst we experience as life slowly slips away without anything noble or deeply fulfilling happening; the relentless mechanical march to the finish line over a course that is disappointingly short; and the economic forces that prevent us from stopping to smell the roses along the path of life. Billy Graham was asked to define life with one word and the word he chose was "brevity." A short life snuffed out by death, the portion of all mankind, provides the raw material for many poems that deal with death or that discuss the intelligent use of time -- the *sine qua non* of a good life.

Much of our time on earth is consumed by the mundane tasks of daily existence, the surface necessities that keep us afloat. At some point on our journey, most of us dig a little deeper and look *just below the surface* as I have tried to do in these poems. In part one, I address the puzzles of life in poems entitled "Death," "Destiny," "Eternity," and other poems on the experiences we choose during the few short years we are given. Life is, after all, a brief period of time during which we experience phenomena, and the phenomena we choose or exclude and how we experience them determine the quality of our brief stay on planet earth. This issue, central to my interest in the puzzles of life, is the focus of the poem entitled "Time" that appears in this book. The following abbreviated version of that poem captures the point I am making better than another paragraph of prose:

> Our rhythms beat to nature's tune
> Chords of life time cycles of moon
> Nature's notes ring in our minds
> Human lives quartz crystals grind
>
> Plant whistle blows a chilling blast
> Humans consumed in minutes per task
> Lawyers bill in tenths of an hour
> Metronome packaged reasoning power
>
> Is opera's aria by the minute heard
> When flamingos fly time we the bird
> Does a violin thrill in parts of an hour
> Or a crescendo chill in fragmented power
>
> At Walden's Pond time was a stream
> In dribbled drops we spill our dream
> Why measure life by sifting sands
> Or in tiny bits ticked off by hands

Mankind craves happiness and no institution is as essential to that end as God's gift of family, especially the love we share with our partner on life's journey. In part two of *Just Below the Surface,* we move from poems probing the puzzles of life to poems focusing on the joy of family, including the family we grow up in and the children, grandchildren, and great-grandchildren that arrive during our adult years.

I grew up in a close family of eight children; family has always been the center of our lives, the source of our joy, the people who share with us the miracle of birth, the pall of death, and events in between. My poems address these events, beginning with the poem "Family" and moving on to "Our Greatest Blessings" (children), "Sisters," and poems about birth, death, community, and married love. Family, if anywhere, is the place where we find ourselves at home in this puzzling world and at peace when we inevitably come to the end of our journey.

Poems are born in the warp and woof of our existence, arise from the raw material of life, and speak to the way we care and the things we share. The meaning of poems (and also of life) is often found *just below the surface*, a place I visited often in writing these poems. I hope you enjoy reading them as much as I have enjoyed writing them.

Rich Wilbur

Puzzles of Life

Books

Books, not dogs, are man's
best friends
Companions for life from
beginning to end

Books feed our minds and
nourish our souls
They challenge us to seek
the highest goals

Best friends at the least
perhaps a bit more
Books burrow and bore,
meld with our core

A book traces events to
the earliest ages
Trips to all nations exist
on its pages

A social event, a solitary activity,
either way, a compelling proclivity
Reading alone with rain on the roof
time speeds by like a horse's hoof

A traveling companion, a tour guide,
font of knowledge, directing the ride
A pleasant itch of quiet anticipation
curiosity – the source of creation

Confinement

Is there a purpose to an
illness that prolongs
Does it fit a cosmic plan
to silence my life's song

Is a lesson taught by a
life of constant pain
My journey confined
to a sliver of a lane

Is character refined raising
fences like a pen
Where I can only know the
places I have been

How do I adjust to the
disability cage
What lines do I write
on my blank page

Abundant possibilities His
providence provides
The gift of grace assures He
is always by my side

At last the book of life turns
its final page
No blank sheet remains as He
opens up my cage

Write a new beginning, next
a middle, last an end
Plow down the fetid fences
confining like a pen

Death

Death's proud democracy
includes aristocracy
The young and the old
the meek and the bold

Hounds the humble poor
beckons the bawdy boor
Casts his random pall
blindfolded over all

For three score and ten
we all have a yen
But death takes no care
to give each his share

Man sees in horror
a certain tomorrow
Decked out on a bier
viewed by a peer

Recoils from the sight
of life's final night
No man slips the glare
of death's deadly stare

Destiny

A poem is a frown at the
puzzle of existence
A furrow in the brow –
inquisitive persistence

Are we a mystic roll
of the genetic dice
Do numbers turned up
spell nasty or nice

Does the creator of all
shuffle the cards
Draw from the pack
to set our odds

Are we biological machines
of unlimited potential
Or are circumstances of birth
the all consequential

Whatever the role of
nature and nurture
Effort determines the
shape of our future

Eternity

born billions of years beyond the big bang,
surfacing in an ocean of oblivion for a brief

gasp of life, five billion surfaced with me,
inhaling, exhaling, expiring, sinking under

again, forever, five billion bodies built of
parts so identical in form and function

that medical mechanics use the same tool
box to fix five billion bladders, like

Goodwrench fixing flats or replacing points
and plugs, the same models, the same manuals.

still, sometimes, when soaping my arms in the
shower, toweling sweat from my face, jogging

on a runner's high or swimming laps in a groove,
I am startled by the sense of my own body.

the singular solitude of my separate self.

alone.

unique.

one of five billion.

one of one.

Faith and Doubt

suffice it not to be just and kind
why this conflict of heart and mind
we live in a world oft so cruel
is this flawed vessel God's own tool

some think that we are Thine elect
who face a world of benign neglect
reason slides down slippery slope
deprives our soul of precious hope

but who can see the other side
out beyond this earthly ride
with doubting Thomas we oft agree
Lord if there, please help me see

Paul believed spite his unbelief
send me, Lord, the same relief
we trek the earth a forlorn waif
yet Nicodemus was saved by faith

a wrinkled face 'neath hair of gray
old age creeps on us day by day
is an eternal surprise at work within
will a little child be saved from sin

seeking we wait for the returning tide
faith our guide on the heaven bound ride
faith and doubt still fight their war
will faith win out as we near God's shore

Freedom

can freedom write
a single line
of rules imposed the
pen be blind

is ego the ink of
every poem
does habit hack and
hew the stone

do the lines read a
page of heart
or by ritual recite
the social part

is a poem from me
for me alone
or the spiral web of
society clone

Grace

Deep in the soul lies the
residence of Grace
A house of many mansions
respite from the race

Living in our heart is the
rose we know as Love
A flutter of her petal lifts
our eyes to things above

Grace and Love are neighbors
so near are heart and soul
Their progeny dwell nearby
and play a starring role

What are the children's names
the fruits of Grace and Love:
Piety, Pardon, Prayer, Peace
the last in form a dove

Gratitude

Gratitude is an attitude
centered in our core
Just a little kindness will
open wide the door

Gratitude is a verbal smile
lips talking from the heart
Followed by a thank you
--the important part

Gratitude is mind in motion
seeing every kindness
Uttering empty platitudes
amounts to social blindness

Gratitude comes so natural
eliminates the strife
Wrap your arms around it
make it part of life

He Will Set It Right

In the stillness of the evening
feel the footsteps of the Lord
In the music of the morning
hear Him strike a perfect chord

Be unearthly quiet in the
nothingness of night
As the author of your life
in silence sets it right

We reset the clock of time
from the date of His birth
Measure molecules in motion
by His time upon the earth

Let all the choirs of angels
sing the glory of His might
Ring all the bells of earth
for the lighting of His light

Can we not hold this Babe in
the bosom of our heart
His life transforming presence
fire for us a new start

Housebound

Freedom is a slender stone
    chipped by custom
    eroded by ego
    hardened by habit

Creativity stirs in every soul
    clipped by conformity
    annulled by approval
    eclipsed by expectation

A kitten lurks in every heart
    declawed
    neutered
    littered

      Housebound

Inside-Out

the pattern of life you
cut to measure
the fit reflects the things
you treasure

all men are tailors sewing
each day
suturing the seams to find
our way

most take their fashion from
outside-in
the latest wrinkle covers
their skin

a few like Thoreau cut
inside-out
the head monkey in Paris
has no clout

look in the mirror what cloth
do you see
is it all that you can and want
to be

the garment is life you cut
and measure
it always reflects the things
you treasure

Kindness

The power of Mother Nature
engenders fear and awe
Survive one of her eruptions
fear less a mauling claw

Power comes from coal and oil
energy from the sun
Splitting of the mighty atom
explosions from a gun

The wind's whistled warning of
an approaching storm
The roiling roar of ocean waves
grown to gigantic form

More powerful than all of nature
from earth to sky above
Is a gentle act of simple kindness
expressing human love

A word of comfort for the weary
overcome by doubt
A tender touch for a sickly man
losing his final bout

A prisoner won his freedom
served all his time
Needs help on reentry lest
he repeat the crime

Share some of your good fortune
with the down and out
The man who really needs a job--
he is not a lazy lout

Help shelter a homeless family
sleeping in their car
Children need a chance in life
in order to go far

Mother Nature is powerful yet
equally as kind
Rest softly on her shoulder if
you are in a bind

Bathed in gentle kindness as she
lowers the setting sun
A blissful breeze, softly soothing --
her work today is done

Mother Nature reclines and rests,
power without measure
She sees an act of human kindness
as our greatest treasure

Living Now

at bygone years regret we cast
why all this focus on the past
things long done oft coil and hiss
is the pain of hell a chance we miss

the future stars in the theater of mind
act two of our play appears more kind
but this misty drama has no script
in act two the stage may be a crypt

the past and the future act as fences
barring joy that speaks to our senses
walking half sleeping on a quarter acre
over the fence is the world of our Maker

the future flows through present to past
no life occurs in the first and the last
learn from the past, plan for the future
look to the present our soul to nurture

Melancholy

We dwell in background sadness
inner tears of soft persistence
Related in some unknown way
to the puzzle of existence

At the surface the joy of family
the warmth of faithful friends
Both of them so essential
to achieving human ends

And children, blessed children
font of endless love
The fruit of a loving marriage
gifts from God above

Just below the surface sits a
simmering apprehension
The contingent nature of life
dread of deadly expectation

Roaming randomly around
the hideous grim reaper
Grisly hand on final curtain
he is its ugly keeper

Yet the beauty of the forest
awe at stars above
Reveal a heavenly father who
bathes us in His love

While we breathe fresh air in
the warmth of the sun
Treasure each precious day 'til
life on earth is done

Slow Down

Life is an account holding the asset called time
spending on the trivial is like spilling fine wine
Trade it for trinkets and run wild on the town
but when it is gone, you move underground

Existence before essence philosophers state
start work on the essence before it's too late
Read some good books, care for your mind
kneel down in prayer, your soul to find

Slow down, take it easy, slice up your day
allow enough time for the come what may
Table the BlackBerry, put down the iPhone
take a deep breath and sound a new tone

Slow down, you need time to unwind
control the stress, stay clear of a bind
Life is short, use it slowly, pick your pace
spread it out, make it last, it is not a race

Slow down, plan your life, use your mind
see the tired, the left-out, treat them kind
Careless use of time is a thing to dread
drain the account and you join the dead

The Battle

the sun slips above the rim of the horizon and squats on
the edge of the earth. dewdrops cling to the battlefield

grass, pinpoint pools of shimmering sunlight. silence is
the midwife of a new day. Crack! rifles sound and

round missiles fly from the threshold of a grass strip.
no traffic downwind, base or final. four soldiers sheath

their weapons, board open vehicles, drive down the strip.
wind whips the enemy flag in the distance. Big Bertha

is silent. Traffic! formation of four on final. wide
wing spans of steel gray cushion the silent slip from sky

to earth. wheels down, threshold cleared, perfect landing.
Crack! rifles sound and four round missiles land near

the enemy flag. three soldiers sheath their weapons.

the fourth soldier replaces a divot. a family of four
sandhill cranes clap their wings in the gallery.

The Hourglass of Existence

Birthdays – the hourglass
of our existence
A day you are happy by
unanimous insistence

A day we all hope will be
filled with laughter
When we bury all worry
of the hereinafter

But the burial imposes
a heavy toll
On the center of being--
our human soul

In managed care we
rest our souls
A deluge of details
drowns our goals

Birthdays are for nursing
the center of being
Take no more steps without
really seeing

Look at the few grains of
sand that remain
Dump the deluge of detail
real life regain

What mundane daily tasks
make you want to rant
What do you want to do
that time says you can't

These questions are the map
to the road up ahead
Answer them right or we are
already half-dead

Birthdays – the hourglass
of our existence
The sand is slipping away
in steely persistence

The Mortuary

stately home on North Notre Dame
classic décor from aristocracy came
the rich arrived for a fancy ball
society's best loved to call

soon the history of this abode
turned down a different road
society's best still dying to call
covered with velvet under a pall

a visit is now an awful curse
the limousine a big black hearse
head of the house a trained mortician
keeper of the books a grim statistician

guest of honor is completely calm
beyond the help of Gilead's balm
finely dressed for an evening wake
guests served trays of coffee and cake

the organ plays near the golden dome
"Jesus is tenderly calling me home"
His arms open not to an extra point
but to welcome a soul and him anoint

at Memorial Hospital a few blocks south
a cry is heard from a new babe's mouth
some are departing while others arrive
on North Notre Dame God's plan is alive

Time

born of earth's diurnal turns
for day and night creation yearns
the planet tilts, seasons to bring
months slip by, summer to spring

the moon dances round our sphere
at changing faces mortals peer
our rhythms beat to nature's tune
chords of life time cycles of moon

time and motion studies abound
each sixty seconds gets a pound
plant whistle blows a chilling blast
humans consumed in minutes per task

doctors learned in the healing art
sell ten minutes in a medical mart
lawyers bill in tenths of an hour
metronome packaged reasoning power

typists are clocked in words per minute
letters are quarter notes hit on a spinet
while nature's notes ring in our mind
human lives quartz crystals grind

why by stopwatch do we view
a stunning sunset or pas de deux
by the hands of a sweeping clock
view a rainbow or see a peacock

is opera's aria by the minute heard
when flamingos fly time we the bird
does a violin thrill in parts of an hour
or a crescendo chill in fragmented power

at Walden's Pond time was a stream
in dribbled drops we spill our dreams
why measure life by sifting sand
in tiny bits ticked off by hands

in eternal darkness a candle burns
sustaining life as the planet turns
measure life by the warmth of the sun
the candle flickers and life is done

The Joy of Family

Family

A family is a collection
of God-given friends
Bonded by love until
our journey ends

Creatures produced by the
same human love
From two who are one by
decree from above

Thousands of meals from
the same human table
Sharing stories of our day
long before cable

Raised together in the same
loving home
With them in your life you
are never alone

Where ever you fall on
the face of the planet
Family will be there--
rock solid granite

Wallow in joy with these
special relations
Gathering together gives
lasting elation

An ocean of relationships
exists on the earth
Most important is family
beginning at birth

Our Greatest Blessing

The greatest blessing we have
on earth
Is when our children appear
at birth

Our spirits soar when they
stand and walk
It thrills our soul when they
start to talk

And now the child walks
to school
Where God provides him
every tool

Reading and writing they
learn with speed
Computers and Wi-Fi arrived
in their seed

Before we know it the teens
are driving
We worry each trip about
them surviving

We are saving a bunch to
pay the bill
As college appears just
over the hill

Four years of college slip
by so fast
Living with us now a thing
in the past

The degrees they earn make us
ever so proud
As they move to new space we
cry out loud

Our child bonds with their
lifelong love
Blessed with grace from
God above

They are joined together as
husband and wife
Twain in one flesh for all
of their life

The greatest blessing we have
on earth
Is when our grandchild appears
at birth

Otisville

Kind of like a Field of Dreams
but in a different place
A little mountain village with a
very special grace

Where the young were taught
of God above
And lines of class were blurred
by love

Where right and wrong were
concepts of clarity
Neighbors far more than
objects of charity

The children grew up and
all drifted away
Many years later they
gathered one day

Lines and wrinkles now
frame the face
Yet stamped there still is
that special place

A quiet contentment joins
the setting sun
The peace we share in a
job well done

Blessed be the tie that binds
the people sing
Mystic chords of memory
forever ring

Sisters

the highest form of
life on earth
are perfect at their
date of birth

what names do these
creatures carry
are they unnamed forms
of a celestial fairy

but you know their
names already mister
these perfect creatures
we call sisters

perhaps you remember
sis a few years old
with the natural skills
her future foretold

those skills that make
our sisters great
the reasons they inhabit
this special state

here are a few that
come to mind ----
soft, sweet, gentle
ever so kind

their love a mighty river
that overflows its banks
raining rivulets of love and
all who drink give thanks

are you sick and need
some tending
sister's love will lead
to mending

in finding lost things
all men are blind
no matter the place
sis has it in mind

your ego is growing at
an obnoxious rate
she firmly returns you
to a rational state

you slip and spill
make a mess
she comes and helps
loves you no less

sisters have a sense
of the wholly other
God preparing them
for the role of mother

sisters are heart and soul
of every clan
kindness is their calling
love their plan

Sharon Lee

Sharon is a precious pearl
loving, generous, kind
Needs no one else can see
she always kept in mind

She had to grow up fast
in the turmoil of the time
With little ones to love,
a tender heart so kind

As all her siblings know
she was within her heart
A mother, daughter, sister
and excelled in every part

God looked within her soul
planted there a special grace
Only a few like her He calls
she is rare among the race

She passed this special grace
deep down her family tree
Her children share this grace
as all who know them see

Now is the time to ask as
we are far along the road
What is the final account
gain or loss the child's load

Gain! A glorious return for
while age has slowed her pace
Lines of time cannot obscure
her enduring special grace

Big House Ghosts

born and raised in a country town
it harbors a tale all will astound
walk end to end in less than an hour
pass Plain Cemetery, dead's last bower

planted north, the house of Claus
at the other end, the Big House
lonely quarter mile aside the road
tombstones line up, trouble forebode

leisurely stroll on a sunny day
slow walk too under skies of gray
a different trip on a starless night
curtain of black, skin crawls in fright

no street light glows piercing the dark
have only the dead, my path to mark
a faraway light is the only sign
the Big House waits, safe and benign

eerie apparition appears by my hip
ghost of a greyhound, speed for the trip
the tombstones in fog line our lane
pitch black sky weeps chilling rain

Mercury is back from leading the dead
in numinous awe the essence of dread
to each sneaker the god adds a wing
ready to run, for comfort I sing

out of the blocks with a burst of speed
under my breath the Apostle's Creed
tombstones close, bony hands in check
greyhound's ghost runs neck and neck

running for home to the arms of mother
slipping the orb of the wholly other
nether world on the margins of sight
eyes straight ahead limit the fright

new world record in the quarter mile
but safe at home wearing a smile
greyhound's ghost back up the pike
ready to run the next ghoulish hike

Wayne

A child's silk skin no sign of a line
promise of youth for a life so fine
A life to write on a slate that's clean
with a mind his teachers see as keen

A big league pitcher perhaps we see
throws the baseball hard with glee
He threads the needle --atta boy--
strike three his parents cry with joy

Runs in the woods and trips on a log
licking his wounds, his faithful dog
Crisp red leaves gently break his fall
he stands back up -- a growin tall

Maybe it's a track star that he'll be
the modern version of Wes Santee
A football hero anchoring tight end
a man of steel refusing to bend

Man needs more than a mass of muscle
for life after games is one tough tussle
Sports his ego will massage and caress
his keen young mind school must address

But fate now unfolds a terrible tale
when all of our dreams begin to fail
While walking gaily home from school
our boy is run down by a drunken fool

His battered body prone in the gutter
siblings in shock speak with a stutter
The doctor arrives to battle with fate
reading his face, it's already too late

The problem of evil theologians debate
they have an answer – not so great
His death is part of a world with free will
theologians drinking too much from a still

The moon rises bright in a clear fall sky
a cool wind dries tears of a mother's cry
To heaven she looks for answers to grief
a twinkling new star she glimpses so brief

Existence fore essence philosophers note
at a time like this a miserable quote
A dear young life hardly out of the gate
a cruel act of fate wipes clean the slate

Miracle

a baby boy fresh from the womb
unbounded love surfeits the room
awestruck by the miracle of creation
parents hold hands in mystical elation

the child grows a little each year
again the parents blessed with cheer
the home is now in a constant whirl
as the boy is joined by a baby girl

neither child is very often sick
their growing up too darn quick
headed to school one fine fall day
promoted a grade the following May

mad hatter's cookbook, Goldie's board
collecting stamps and what a hoard
playing baseball and music lessons
doing studies and practice sessions

cycling, camping, off to the shore
grandparents come, our spirits soar
soon followed by a loving sigh
the kids are off to junior high

high school years go by so fast
college graduation here at last
kids are grown and on their own
gifts from God, the form a loan

now I see them but twice a year
thankful the phone keeps us near
the distance fails to dim our love
angels surprise, news from above

settling down with a wife in marriage
son reports they will need a carriage
his father will be a grandpa at last
in the role of aunt daughter is cast

again we await the miracle of creation
lovers hold hands in mystical elation
all anxiously await the joyous new birth
this child will be the best one on earth

Ryan Richard

the door to nowhere
swings both ways
inside the door we
spend our days

says "Exit" above
the side we see
it opens out for
you and for me

a mystery unfolds
on the other side
through the door
Ryan Richard glides

a miniature miracle
this precious new being
no one can doubt
creation we're seeing

from a warp in time
a wormhole in space
our precious new boy
joins the human race

Sean Patrick

This message is one part poem
the other part petition
Please recognize a miracle
despite its repetition

The miracle repeated is the
joy of a new birth
Sean Patrick, Ryan's brother,
born on planet earth

But Sean is not a copy of
his brother head to toe
He has a genetic fingerprint
his special boat to row

Science assembles the pieces
into a coherent whole
But says absolutely nothing
about the human soul

But the totality of this child
emerges from his soul
Unique through all of time
created for this role

So welcome to Sean Patrick
a boy unlike any other
Although his dearest friend
that includes his brother

Thank you, Lord, for the
greatest of all miracles
Your gift of family makes
us positively lyrical

Emma Lynn

Heaven sends a blue-eyed angel
once every thousand years
We delight in her perfection
through a blur of tears

A silk thread sewn divinely in the
seamless web of life
A celestially delivered presence
born to drum and fife

Her beauty blends with power
from the very start
She commands a mighty army
all who lost their heart

Soldiers fall in line, prepare
an about-face
This is a new kind of battle
the general in lace

Where Love and Kindness are
instruments of command
Grace and Peace the weapons
of her final stand

Hannibal, Alexander, Napoleon
lastly Robert Lee
Historians insist they are the best
we will ever see

But o'er the field of battle, amid
the deafening din
A new Joan appears in power
name of Emma Lynn

Caitlin Rose

We believe in miracles
you need only pray
From nothing a few months ago
Caitlin Rose appeared today

A special space in family life
she came forth to fill
From tiny seed to human being
perfected by God's will

Out of nowhere a script unscrolls
new lines on a blank page
And heaven sends our little star
to act on center stage

Sent from Central Casting
perfect for the part
Her role is sure to win
a place in every heart

Death Do Us Part

Death is restless in repose
we the living feel
Two lives God joined together
sail opposite sides the keel

The ship sails vast and empty
as we drift along alone
Cresting wave and crossing trough
to reach our final home

But there are others on this trip
who wrap me in their coat
They mend the sails and tend the ship
keep me lovingly afloat

Sail on, my love, in mystery
rest in the promised land
Look to the far horizon where
again I'll hold your hand

Jean

In vain I wish to
know you whole
To pass through all
and meet your soul

Bore to core – past
marrow and bone
And strike at last
the corner stone

The gentle touch
caressing words
The sweetest tones
in softest chords

The smile that rarely
leaves your lips
The pique you show
by hands on hips

You are slow to anger
quick to cool
Will not be bound
by silly rule

From command center
that runs our show
A perfect performance--
we love you so

Sharing

spirit down to skin and bone
trekking the road of life alone
worn and weary, wandering astray
a chance encounter saved my day

we met under a clear night sky
'twas a perfect fit without a try
who was it led me first to greet
and then to marry a girl so sweet

now she is my greatest treasure
a mate I love beyond all measure
I share with her this earthly ride
straying not from her dear side

soon we cross the bridge of sighs
and dwell forever beyond the sky
He who gave us life and love
will bid us welcome from above

until that day we all will face
with joy we run this earthly race
spent we'll reach the finish line
share our love through all of time

A Lifelong Event

Mass-produced love on a
prepackaged page
Commercial valentines
started the craze

Everyone does it regardless
of mood --
Put a card in the cart along
with the food

Love in a splash of store
bought color
BJ's will say it as cheap
as a dollar

Love on command is a
mistake, not a crime
But it is better expressed
in spontaneous time

When the Love of your life
looks that certain way
That stopped your heart on
a long-ago day

When she tilts her head, that
smile on her face
The one that starts your
heart to race

Hands on her hips with that
soft loving glance
One of a kind charm, leaving
you in a trance

Then love overflows as soft
as a breath
I will love you my Dearest
until my death

The Reasons for My Love

I love you for the tears you shed
warmly for my pain
The troubled turmoil of your toil
only for my gain

I love the gentle kindness you
reserve for every friend
Who know you will be with them
until they reach the end

I love you for your grasp of things
ordered and in place
Brightened by your sense of humor
the smile upon your face

I love you for the path you found
to His redeeming grace
Walking with me along the path
beyond this senseless race

And I love you for you alone
God's one and only you
For teaching me, despite my faults
God can love me too

Called

The door of existence
slides open a crack
A baby slips through
the welcome a whack

I'll fight you bastards
she bellows at birth
And elbows her way
to the top of the earth

A horizon of glory
spreads out like a psalter
The valley is a nave
the plain is an altar

A choir of birds sings
in a mountain cathedral
An angel appears on
a tree for a steeple

She sinks to her knees
in awe on her perch
Oh Lord my God
the earth is a church

She trades her elbows for
a pair of clasped hands
And prays on her knees
for peace in all lands

The Love Between Us

You know for sure they are
a mother and a child
By traits common to humans
and pets no longer wild

The same hair or eyes or the
color of the skin
The way they tilt their head
a dimple on the chin

Or is there something larger
difficult to see
Ineffable way of sharing, like
the verb "to be"

We need a larger canvas than
eyes and hair and skin
Far beyond specifics like a
dimple on a chin

Yes, an ineffable way of being
on earth and above
The only essential element
unconditional love

The mother here is homo sapiens
the child feline genus
Yet mother and child bound
by the love between us

The Star

the family acts together
when she directs the play
choreographs our daily drama
from center stage each day

sent from Central Casting
and perfect for the part
she wins an Academy Award
performing the mother's art

a repertoire of endless roles
nurse, teacher, mother, saint
the leading lady of our stage
and a pretty portrait to paint

the CEO of Canberley Drive
the place that we call home
this script is from my heart
my love is etched in stone

My Silver Queen

A quarter of a century--
a third of my life
Tucked in the arms of
my precious wife

Our silver anniversary
break out the wine
Use the fine china as
together we dine

We are going for gold
unaware of our age
Just taking each day
and turning the page

Silver is a waypoint of
our loving marriage
We continue our journey
bring 'round the carriage

Put away the silver, bring
on the gold
Many more years, my love
I can hold

My Lady, My Wife

People use love as an
all-purpose term
Flowering foliation—
a fern on a berm

They wallow in the ooze
of listless abstraction
Love in this sense is
cloying distraction

Real love permeates the
core of our being
An emotional osmosis
related to seeing

And what I see is the
love of my life
The beautiful lady who
became my wife

Thoughtful and Kind
Generous and Tender
Slender and Curvaceous
no mistaking her gender

Kindness for others God
stamped on her soul
So many she has helped--
a long roll to call

Today is silver plus one
no need to discuss age
Our love keeps growing--
turn one more page

My Queen Still Reigns

A quiet resignation rules the
kingdom of her face
Reigns in gritty determination
to renew again the race

The border of her country is
shrinking year by year
Soldiers fall in battle, her
pain anoints their biers

Each pound of flesh carries
a heavy load of pain
But the microbial marauders
wage this war in vain

For she has an air of sweetness
hopeful as a hymn
Queen of my horizon, her
battle never dims

Time and Tradition

Ivy hugs a red brick wall
Moss clings to gray garden stone
Whispers of time and tradition

The schools we attend
Like the church of our youth
Shape our very being

Love of a favorite book
The peace of an hour in prayer
Nurse child to adult

Mom, Dad, Sister, Brother
Bond, blend, become part of us
We forever part of them

We fall deeply in love
Then become twain in one flesh
Create our time and tradition

The End

The End is a stop for rest
on the highway of eternity
Last page of a poetry book
born of modest paternity

The End is a time of reflection
on places we have been
When we plan a new beginning
early mistakes we mend

The End is a compass bearing
at an intersection of life
We head in a new direction
without the stress and strife

The End is a point to realize
we have done the best we can
And enjoy a quiet satisfaction
with the resilient race we ran

CPSIA information can be obtained
at www.ICGtesting.com
Printed in the USA
BVHW031153060620
580989BV00004B/9/J

9 781478 723035